OLD BONES

The Wonder Horse

By MILDRED MASTIN PACE

Illustrated by Wesley Dennis

SCHOLASTIC BOOK SERVICES

NEW YORK · TORONTO · LONDON · AUCKLAND · SYDNEY · TOKYO

Published by Scholastic Book Services, a division
of Scholastic Magazines, Inc., New York, N.Y.

TO ALL THOSE, YOUNG AND OLD, WHO KNEW THE GREAT THOROUGHBRED, EXTERMINATOR, AND REMEMBER HIM WITH LASTING AFFECTION AND ADMIRATION

Copyright © 1955 by Mildred Mastin Pace and Wesley Dennis. This edition is published by Scholastic Book Services, a division of Scholastic Magazines, Inc., by arrangement with Whittlesey House, a division of the McGraw-Hill Book Company, Inc.

7th printing . . . . August 1974

Printed in the U.S.A.

CONTENTS

1 READY TO RUN

The big horse sniffed the cool spring air and whinnied happily. It was a clear, silvery April morning, a fine morning for running. It made the horse feel good.

He snorted in high spirits and ran to the end of the paddock. He turned his head in the direction of the track. Oh, he could have kicked up his heels, cleared the fence, and lit out alone! For he knew the way. But he didn't go. He stood waiting, feeling the pale warmth of the sun on his back, sniffing the air that was as sweet and fresh as spring water, nibbling a little at the new grass drenched with dew.

Soon the exercise boy came, the saddle was put in place, and they were ready to go.

The minute they hit the track the horse knew that this morning the rider was going to give him his head, let him run as he wished. That he loved! Down the stretch he pounded, faster—the strides strengthening, lengthening—faster, faster. As fast as he wanted to go — nothing, nobody, holding him back. It was almost as good as running in a race. Well, at least it was the next best thing. He hadn't had a chance to run in a race for quite some time now. Meanwhile, this would have to do.

He ran joyously, as if he would never stop. And when

he did stop, his breathing was still light and steady, and he felt as if he could have gone on and on, running, never tiring, never breaking the rhythm of the running.

For three mornings in a row now, a man had leaned on the fence and watched him run. The horse did not know the man. This morning the man left the fence and followed the horse and exercise boy back to the barn.

In the barn the grooms and other stable help treated the man with great respect. They said, "Morning, Mr. McDaniel. . . . How are you, Mr. McDaniel? How is Sun Briar, Mr. McDaniel?"

Mr. McDaniel was one of the most famous race-horse trainers in the country. He was the trainer of the beautiful thoroughbred Sun Briar, the horse favored to win the Kentucky Derby.

Now the men asked, "You feel sure Sun Briar will win the Derby, Mr. McDaniel? Sure is a handsome horse, Sun Briar, isn't he, Mr. McDaniel?"

While he answered their questions and talked to the men, Mr. McDaniel's eyes never left the big horse he had followed into the barn. He was an awkward-looking animal, with bones jutting angularly under his chestnut coat. But Mr. McDaniel saw, too, the strong lines of his well-shaped head, the wisdom and understanding in the wide-set eyes.

One of the grooms laughed and said, "How come you're looking at big Old Bones here? Ugliest thorough-bred anywhere around, he is."

Mr. McDaniel said, "That his name? Old Bones? But he isn't old, is he?"

"No, he's a three-year-old. Matter of fact, won't have **his** third birthday till the end of May. We just call him

Old Bones on account of how he looks. His real name is Exterminator. But so far he hasn't lived up to his name." The men laughed.

"Exterminator?"

"Yes, sir. Mr. Cal Milam owns him. He bought him as a yearling and had great hopes for him. Brought him home and asked Mrs. Milam to name him. Said this colt was going to grow up into a big, strong race horse. Told her to give him a name that would say he was going to kill off all competition. So she named him Exterminator."

Mr. McDaniel put a gentle hand on the big horse's bony withers. The horse liked the touch of his hand. He sniffed at the man's shoulder and bumped his nose against it. Mr. McDaniel smiled and rubbed the big creature's head.

"Hasn't done much exterminating though." The groom shrugged. "Only ran four races all told—lost two.

Hasn't raced at all this year."

Mr. McDaniel rubbed the horse's muzzle and said, "He surely is well mannered. Quietest thoroughbred I think I ever saw." Then he said good-by to the men and turned to leave.

Old Bones whinnied softly after him. He had liked his touch, the sound of his voice. McDaniel gave him a firm pat and said softly, so softly only the horse heard him, "I hope to be back, fella. Wish me luck."

A groom, following him to the barn door said, "Yes, he's quiet. But most folks don't think much of him on account of his looks."

Old Bones was used to being told he was ugly, homely. For almost three years now—since the day he was born—he had been called ugly.

The people who came to look at him when he was only a few hours old talked about it. "How," they asked, "how in the world could a dam as beautiful as Fair Empress and a sire as handsome as McGee produce this scarecrow of a foal?"

"Looks like he's built of kindling wood—nothing but bones!"

"Maybe he'll grow up to his bones," it was hopefully suggested.

"No, this kind never does. He'll be nothing but bones all his life. Just bones."

That was when they began calling him Bones. The other foals had names that described them, too. They were names like Star and Velvet, Little Bay, Beauty, and Blaze. They were pet names, given in admiration. But Bones was a homely name for a poor little homely foal.

Once it looked as if the men were going to try to make

him better-looking. That was when he was a year old. He was put in a paddock alone, rubbed and curried and brushed, and given special mashes to fatten him up.

But a groom, brushing him, said, "A man can't make pearly gates out of a mud fence. I can't make you look good, but you'll look your best when we take you up to Saratoga to be sold."

A few weeks later, at Saratoga, waiting to be auctioned off, scared, facing the biggest crowd of people he had ever seen, he heard, "Homely, isn't he? . . . Looks like he's built of tent poles. . . . Not much to look at, I say." And when the auctioneer banged down his gavel and yelled, "Sold! For fifteen hundred dollars . . . ," the crowd buzzed, "Not bad for that colt—not a big price, but not bad for such a homely one."

In spite of Bones' appearance, his new owner had great plans for him. He made Bones feel proud. But in the spring Bones became ill. Not until an operation was performed did he begin to gain strength. It was the end of June before he was able to run his first race.

The day of his first race! What a great day that had been. Bones had never known such exhilaration, such pure joy! The second of tense quiet before the break, the burst of speed at the start, the running with the pack surrounded by thunder—pulling away, forcing more strength, more speed into the lengthening strides — the final burst of speed at the finish . . . the roars from the grandstands, the jockeys' cries. Oh, this was why he had been born—to run like this!

Three more times in the fall he ran — three glorious, wonderful times. Then he came up lame. He had not raced since.

Now he was a three-year-old, and few people had ever heard of Exterminator. Many who had known his name had forgotten he had ever raced.

But Exterminator had not forgotten. Whenever he heard the bugle announce post time, telling everyone a race was about to begin, he stood alone in his stall, trembling, hoping, waiting—his ears twitching, his breath coming faster. No, he would never forget.

A groom came with fresh water. "What on earth is Mr. Henry McDaniel looking you over for?" he asked. "Man like that's not hanging 'round a horse without something on his mind."

Old Bones whinnied, but this didn't give the groom an answer.

2   MR. KILMER
BUYS A HORSE

When Henry McDaniel left Old Bones, there were two men he had to see. The first was his boss, Mr. Kilmer, the man who owned Sun Briar.

Mr. Kilmer was a man of great wealth. He could have almost anything that money could buy. Right now the thing he wanted most in the world was to see Sun Briar win the Kentucky Derby. Money could not buy that. But it could help.

Mr. Kilmer had already spent a great deal of money to make his wish come true. He had paid six thousand dollars for Sun Briar when the horse was one year old. In the two years that followed he had spent many thousands more to give the colt the best of care, the finest training. He was as sure as a man could be that Sun Briar would win the Derby.

Mr. McDaniel admired Sun Briar, too. The colt was one of the fastest and handsomest thoroughbreds he had ever trained. It was his dream, too, to see Sun Briar win the Derby.

But Mr. McDaniel was an honest man. He was so honest he sometimes seemed tough. He loved horses, and he knew horses. He had been born on a race track. He could not remember when he had not worked with horses. His father, who had owned and trained thoroughbreds had taught him how to handle them from the time Henry could walk.

When Henry McDaniel looked at a horse, he looked without prejudice. He did not see what he wished to see or what he hoped to see. He saw what he saw. And he saw truly. Now he saw that Sun Briar was not training as well as he should.

Mr. McDaniel went to Mr. Kilmer. He said, "I don't want to upset you, but I think you should know that Sun Briar isn't doing his best in training. When we exercise him, he doesn't run as fast as he should. I think he needs a work horse. If he had a work horse running with him, I believe he would run better."

Mr. Kilmer said, "If you need a work horse to bring Sun Briar up to top condition, by all means get one. You should be able to get a work horse for six or seven hundred dollars."

Mr. McDaniel winced. He knew he could not buy the work horse he had in mind for seven hundred dollars.

He said, "We need a rather special work horse, Mr. Kilmer. Sun Briar is a fast colt. The work horse will have to have speed, too. He will have to set a fast pace for Sun Briar, or the workouts will be useless."

"Naturally." Mr. Kilmer sounded impatient.

"Also," Mr. McDaniel said, "we need an animal that is quiet and well mannered. Sun Briar is very high-strung and excitable. The work horse must have a calm disposition."

"Of course. Get one. I still say you can find such an

animal for around seven hundred dollars. However, if you can't—well, do your best. But get what Sun Briar needs."

There was no use arguing. Mr. Kilmer was already saying good-by to the trainer.

Next Mr. McDaniel went to see Mr. Cal Milam, Exterminator's owner. He told Mr. Milam, honestly, that he was interested in buying Old Bones as a work horse for Sun Briar. What was the price?

Mr. Milam frowned. "I'm not anxious to sell him. I've always felt he would race well someday. Now you want him for a work horse."

"Yes. A work horse for Sun Briar." There was an uncomfortable silence. Then Mr. McDaniel said, "He hasn't made much of a record as a race horse."

"That is true," Mr. Milam said. "But I thought enough of him, even so, to nominate him for this year's Kentucky Derby."

Mr. McDaniel smiled. "That doesn't mean much. Sixty-nine horses were nominated for this year's Derby, and only ten are scheduled to run. He hasn't raced all year."

Mr. Milam said, "Well, anyhow, I wouldn't sell him cheap. I wouldn't sell him for less than twelve, thirteen thousand dollars."

Mr. McDaniel swallowed hard. He pushed the thought of Mr. Kilmer's seven hundred dollars out of his mind. He said, "I couldn't go that high—nine thousand maybe."

"No. I wouldn't take less than twelve."

So they dickered. Mr. McDaniel said, "We have two fillies I could add to the cash price—they're worth at least five hundred each."

Mr. Milam said, "Look here! I'm not eager to sell him.

15

EXTERMINATOR

(OLD BONES)

Since what you want is a work horse, surely you could find another animal for much less money than I'm asking."

Mr. McDaniel shook his head. He couldn't explain why it was so important that he have this horse and no other. But throughout the dickering he could see the horse—big, patient, wise. The fine head, the eyes that almost talked, the soft muzzle gently nudging his arm. This was the horse he must have.

"How about eleven thousand in cash and the two fillies?"

Back and forth they talked.

When Henry McDaniel left Mr. Milam's house, Exterminator's new owner was Mr. Willis Sharpe Kilmer.

Although, as yet, Mr. Kilmer didn't know it.

Before breaking the news to Mr. Kilmer, Henry McDaniel went out to the barns to see the horse he had just bought.

Old Bones was in his stall. He knew McDaniel. He thrust his head toward the man and whinnied a greeting.

It was early afternoon. In the distance a bugle sounded "Boots and Saddles." It was time for the first race at the Lexington track. At the sound Old Bones raised his head sharply. His nostrils quivered, and for a moment he forgot the man standing there.

McDaniel spoke. "You know what that tune means, don't you? Poor fellow! So few races—and none since last fall. But you still remember. You still want to go!"

The bugle call was over, and Bones put his head down for his friend to pet. McDaniel's voice was gentle. "I hope you'll forgive me for what I'm doing to you. Buying you for a work horse. But trust me, fella. We'll see. . . . Meantime we've got to get Sun Briar in peak condition for the Derby. That's our job now. We can't think of anything but Sun Briar now. Understand?"

Mr. Kilmer was remarkably calm when Henry McDaniel told him about the work horse. He said, "But that's more than *fifteen times* what I told you to pay."

"Yes, I know. But I did my best. And you told me to get what Sun Briar needed. I think the work horse is worth what I paid for him."

"Well, you're the trainer. You think he'll really be able to keep Sun Briar on his toes?"

"Yes, I do."

"All right, Henry." Mr. Kilmer smiled. "Anything for Sun Briar."

The next day Sun Briar and his work horse traveled to Louisville. There, two weeks later, at Churchill Downs, the Kentucky Derby would be run.

When the horse van drew up to the barns at Churchill Downs, a group of men waited, watching. Word had got around that the beautiful Sun Briar was arriving.

Everyone wanted to see the thoroughbred that was probably going to win the Kentucky Derby.

Nobody noticed Old Bones when he walked from the van. Except McDaniel. He gave the horse an affectionate pat and watched while a groom led him to the barn.

But when the door of the van opened and Sun Briar stepped out, admiring bursts of sound came from the crowd. For here, indeed, was a prince among colts. The creature arched his beautiful neck and tossed his head back, his eyes brilliant on the crowd. He danced back a few steps, shied, reared high. Every movement was one of exquisite grace. And when he finally allowed the groom to lead him away, he walked as if to music.

In the barn, Mr. Kilmer waited. He looked anxiously at Sun Briar. "He's all right? Didn't get too nervous on the ride over, did he?"

"He's fine," McDaniel assured him.

Mr. Kilmer looked at the other horse that had been led in.

"My word, Henry! Is that ugly thing the work horse you paid all that money for?"

Henry McDaniel nodded.

"The horse must have hypnotized you!" Kilmer growled. But at once his eyes were back on Sun Briar, and nothing could spoil the joy he felt when he looked at that beautiful animal. Now when he spoke, his voice was happy. "You know, Henry, the dream of every man who owns a racing stable is to see a horse of his run in the Kentucky Derby. This year, for the first time, that dream will come true for me." He smiled. "More than that, I think we will win it. I don't believe Sun Briar can fail!"

3   THE WORK HORSE

At first Old Bones did not understand his workouts with Sun Briar.

It was different from anything he had done before. Though he was running with another horse, it was not racing. For, he soon realized, nobody cared whether he finished first. In fact, sometimes his exercise boy held him back so that Sun Briar could run ahead. No, there was none of the exhilaration of the race in this.

Neither was it exercising as he had known it before. And in the workouts—when they ran against time—nobody seemed to care how fast or how slowly he had run the distance. It was puzzling.

Bones had known that Sun Briar wasn't too eager to work out. But then, he was a high-strung colt, a creature of moods. He could run as fast as the wind if he wanted to; Bones was sure of that. And now, suddenly, Bones realized what his own job was—to make Sun Briar want to run, to do his best to encourage and urge Sun Briar on. It would take a lot of teasing and humoring on Bones' part. But he would try.

Oh, Sun Briar was temperamental. Sometimes he raced best if they ran neck and neck. Often he ran better if Old Bones stayed a length or so behind him, urging him on with the thunder of his hooves.

Other times, if Old Bones stayed behind, Sun Briar slowed up, bored. Then Old Bones plunged ahead, spurring the favorite to come on and take the lead.

Henry McDaniel watched, scarcely daring to believe what he saw.

After a workout he said to the exercise boy riding Old Bones, "Did you slow Exterminator up, there on the stretch, so Sun Briar could pass him?"

"No, sir, Boss. I don't tell this horse nothin' no more." He grinned. "Seems like he knows what Sun Briar needs. I just give him his head."

Then one morning Mr. Kilmer came to watch the workout. The two horses started out at a good clip, running neck and neck. Sun Briar was not too interested. Bones dropped behind, and Sun Briar ran faster. As long as Bones stayed behind, Sun Briar flew! Bones dropped

half a length, a full length, letting the favorite pound faster and faster, happy in the lead.

McDaniel, watching the storm gather in Mr. Kilmer's eyes, wished he could yell to Old Bones, "Take the lead this time, boy, take the lead!" For Exterminator could have, with ease.

McDaniel waited for the roar, and it came. "Henry! That fool work horse can't even keep up with Sun Briar in a workout! You must have been crazy when you bought him. Sell him!"

Henry McDaniel said, "Let me explain—he was holding back on purpose. He—"

"ON PURPOSE? Now I know you've gone crazy."

Mr. McDaniel said steadily, "No. I'm not crazy. Exterminator was letting Sun Briar run ahead."

"Letting him run ahead!" Mr. Kilmer's voice was biting with sarcasm. "Now that is *some* race horse. He *lets* other horses race ahead of him. He *likes* to run behind. Well, I don't want him in my stable. Hear? Sell him! Give him away! But get him off the track. He has no business there."

And Mr. Kilmer was gone.

Later Mr. McDaniel went to the barn to see Bones. "You old wonder, you. You got us both in wrong, doing the right thing, didn't you?" The horse rubbed his head against the trainer's shoulder and listened. "You can't blame Mr. Kilmer—I did sound a little balmy. It's the kind of thing a man won't believe unless he sees. And even then he can't be sure—not at first. . . . Trouble with you is, you're too smart for people."

Time for the Derby grew closer. It was six more days, five more days, four more days. Old Bones continued his

workouts with the favorite.

Men leaned on the fence in the mornings and watched the workouts. They had little interest in the big, homely work horse. They did not see what Henry McDaniel saw. They had eyes only for the beautiful Sun Briar. And most of them said, "He looks good."

Henry McDaniel heard them, and he wished he could agree. But the doubt that had nagged him into buying a work horse for Sun Briar had grown. To him Sun Briar didn't look as good as he should. The fire, the brilliance he had when in top form, was missing.

Three more days till the Derby, two more days.

Then it was Friday, and tomorrow was the race.

Rain fell in a gray drizzle. Henry McDaniel stood in the rain watching Sun Briar and Bones. He felt as dismal as the day.

The rain was already turning the hard-packed track to mud. Sun Briar had not been too enthusiastic when the track was dry. Now he was being finicky about running in the mud.

In spite of his low spirits, McDaniel grinned at Bones. The work horse sloshed merrily through the mud as if it weren't there.

His eyes back on Sun Briar, McDaniel sighed. Maybe he was wrong about him. How he would love to believe that!

Leaning on the fence, not far from McDaniel, another man watched the workout. He was Matt Winn, President of Churchill Downs. He had seen every Kentucky Derby since the first one in 1875. And no man alive knew thoroughbreds better than he did.

McDaniel dreaded to ask the question. But he had to. "How do you think Sun Briar looks, Matt?"

Mr. Winn was quiet for a long minute, then he said slowly, "Sluggish."

McDaniel went back to the barn and waited to watch the groom cool out Sun Briar. The groom walked the horse slowly around the walking ring, letting him sip a little water now and then as he wanted it, walking him slowly, slowly until his breathing became normal. It took quite a little while.

Bones was already back in his stall, munching hay.

When Sun Briar was led to his stall, Mr. McDaniel followed. Sun Briar stood sulkily, not moving toward the rack of fresh hay. McDaniel had thought the day before that he was a little off his feed. The groom read the trainer's thoughts and said, "I don't think he is eating quite as well as he should."

"I was afraid of that." McDaniel shrugged into a raincoat, pulled an old hat down on his head. On his way out he stopped at Bones' stall. Old Bones turned from the hayrack and thrust his head toward McDaniel, happy to see him. McDaniel rubbed the white spot on the high forehead and said, "It's not your fault, heaven knows. You did more than anybody could expect from man or beast. If it had been possible to bring Sun Briar up, you would have done it. It wasn't possible, that's all."

With a heavy sigh he went out into the rain, on his way to see Mr. Kilmer. This was one of the few times Henry McDaniel almost wished he had gone into some other business. He had never dreaded an errand so much.

4 THE EVE
OF THE DERBY

Mr. Kilmer greeted his trainer cheerfully. "Good morning, Henry. How's Sun Briar?"

McDaniel hated to say what he had to say, but there was no use beating around the bush. He said, "Sun Briar is sluggish, Mr. Kilmer. I don't think he should run tomorrow."

"What? Take Sun Briar out of the Derby? Scratch him? Now?"

"That's what I mean," McDaniel said sadly. "I just don't think he's in condition for the Derby."

"I can't believe it! What's wrong with him? What happened?"

"He's sluggish. And off his feed. I don't think he's up to the race. I don't think it would be fair to the horse to race him."

"McDaniel, are you sure? You know what this means to me. Two years of planning and hoping, of work and money have gone into preparing this colt for the Derby."

"I know — I know how much you counted on tomorrow. . . ."

"Others counted on it, too. If we had known sooner, it might not have been so hard to take. But the day before! Why, we have guests from all over the country here to see my colt run. And Mrs. Kilmer's party tonight" —his voice was bitter—"a party to celebrate my first Derby entry. It's fantastic." He looked at McDaniel searchingly. "You *are* sure?"

"Yes, I'm sure. And believe me, Mr. Kilmer, it was a hard decision to make."

There was a long silence; then Mr. Kilmer said, "Well, you're the trainer. You're the man who must decide whether the horse is fit to run or not. If you say he isn't, there's only one thing I can do."

Mr. McDaniel was getting ready to leave when another caller arrived. It was Mr. Matt Winn. He looked at the bleak faces of trainer and owner and said, "I see you've decided to scratch Sun Briar."

"Yes."

"I know this is a shocking disappointment for you, Kilmer. You've counted on Sun Briar for a long time."

"Yes," said Mr. Kilmer. "This is a blow that's hard to take. I've never had a Derby entry before. Knowing the Kilmer colors would be in the race this year has meant a great deal to me. . . ."

Mr. McDaniel felt sorry for Mr. Kilmer. He wished he could think his own judgment might be wrong. But he was sure—Sun Briar was not in condition, and his decision was the right one.

Matt Winn said, "Who was the horse working out with Sun Briar this morning?"

Mr. Kilmer spoke bitterly. "A truck horse named Exterminator. A work horse McDaniel here spent too much of my money for."

Mr. Winn said carefully, "He didn't look bad in the

workout. I thought he looked rather well. Perhaps—"

Mr. Kilmer exploded. "You're not suggesting I put my colors up on that work horse, are you? That horse can't outrun me!" He rose abruptly. "I've had enough for one day!" Angrily he strode out of the room.

Mr. Winn said, "I didn't mean to insult him. Probably a foolish idea—the horse most likely isn't even eligible."

"Yes, he is." Mr. McDaniel spoke eagerly. "Cal Milam nominated him for the Derby. We bought him from Cal. He's eligible all right."

"Well, you're the trainer. What do you think?"

"I think he can run. I had my eye on him some time before we bought him. He's fast and strong. We bought him as a work horse, yes. But I never underestimated his speed. And he's—" Henry McDaniel started to tell Matt Winn more about Old Bones, but thought better of it and finished, "He's the best-natured thoroughbred I ever had anything to do with."

Matt Winn smiled. "You ought to be able to give Kilmer a good sales talk. With Sun Briar out anyhow, he has little to lose. Next to winning the race, of course, Kilmer wants more than anything in the world to see his silk in the Derby. Go talk to him. I'll wait."

At first Mr. Kilmer wouldn't listen to Henry McDaniel. He cut him short angrily. "The suggestion that I run that plug-ugly work horse is the silliest thing I ever heard! Why, he looks as if he's ready to fall apart!"

"He's not handsome, that I know," Mr. McDaniel admitted, "but he's—"

"He can't even run!" Mr. Kilmer interrupted. "Don't forget, I watched him work out. Sun Briar walked away from him."

"He wasn't running then. But he *can* run," McDaniel said stubbornly.

"Bah! He's no race horse." Kilmer's voice rose. "He didn't even do a job as a work horse! He's fit for the livery stable, that's all. And, by gad, that's where I intend to send him!"

McDaniel spoke in desperation. "Mr. Kilmer, you don't know the horse. He has strength, and speed, and—"

"And as much class as a rail fence," Kilmer roared.

"Forget his appearance for a minute. He may not look as if he has any class. *His* class is where you can't see it— inside. He's honest and intelligent. And he's got plenty of heart in that big ramshackle body of his. I won't say he'll win the Derby for you. But I will say he won't disgrace the Kilmer colors if you run him."

Before Kilmer could answer, Matt Winn's voice cut in. He walked into the room saying, "You want your silks up, Kilmer. Run him. If he were my horse, I'd have him in the Derby tomorrow."

"You would?" Kilmer asked, surprised.

"I would indeed."

Mr. Kilmer stared at the two men for a minute, then threw his hands up in the air. "All right! All right! I'm probably a fool to be talked into this, but I'll send the work horse to the post tomorrow instead of to a livery stable."

Reluctantly Willis Kilmer announced that a chestnut gelding named Exterminator would wear the Kilmer colors in the Kentucky Derby.

That evening rain clouds hung low, and darkness fell early. But only the weather was dismal. In Louisville, and for miles around, there was gaiety and merrymaking.

It was the night before the Derby—a night for parties and fun. People had come to Kentucky from all over the nation. Yes, from Canada and from Europe, too. They must see more than the Derby. They must see Kentucky hospitality at its gayest!

Against the dark night the great country houses blazed with light.

Inside the houses, bands played; people danced and sang. The light glittered from chandeliers, shimmered on silken gowns, shone on silver and crystal and gleaming damask. Tables were laid with magnificent feasts—country ham, fried chicken, roast duck, beaten biscuits, cakes and pies, and special puddings. And never did a dish stay empty.

The sounds of music and dancing, song and laughter overflowed the houses, spilled across the fields and meadows, into the night.

In Louisville, too, all doors were opened wide in welcome. There was scarcely a house not filled with guests. People packed the hotels and restaurants and jammed the streets. They crowded lobbies and porches and doorways, and stood in line waiting their turn to get rooms and meals and cabs.

And they talked.

There were hundreds of thousands of people in Louisville that night. Many of them had never seen each other before and would never see each other again. But there were no strangers. They were all friends, for they had one common interest, and talked of one thing: THE DERBY.

The big news, the shocking news, was that Sun Briar would not run.

"Have you heard?" they asked. "Kilmer has scratched Sun Briar. . . . Sun Briar won't run. Isn't that something?"

"I came all the way from California to see Sun Briar win that race. . . . Have you heard? Sun Briar is out of the Derby. . . . Sun Briar is scratched! . . . I came all the way from New York to see that colt take the Derby! . . . Is it true that Kilmer has scratched Sun Briar? . . . Yes, it's true. . . ."

"If Sun Briar isn't in the race, who will win? Who's the favorite now?"

"War Cloud will win. . . . War Cloud is the favorite. . . . No, Escoba will win. . . . You'll see, Escoba will win. . . . I think Viva America will take it. . . . Has American Eagle a chance? . . . What about James T. Clarke? . . . Lucky B. will win it—he likes mud. . . . The track will be muddy. Lucky B. is my choice. . . . What about Sewell Combs? He could win it. . . . Yes, Sewell Combs will be right in there. . . . War Cloud. . . . Viva America. . . . Escoba is sure to win. . . ." So they talked and talked.

Nobody said "Exterminator." Not one person said the name, "Exterminator."

5   BOY MEETS HORSE

It was Derby Day.

Henry McDaniel came into the barn, stomping the mud from his boots, shaking the rain from his cap and jacket.

Once again he had gone out to look at the track. It was as bad as he had thought it would be—thick with gooey mud.

Bones whinnied. McDaniel said, "Yes, I know. You want a full report, don't you? Well, it's muddy. Very muddy." He put an arm across Exterminator's withers and rubbed the long, sloping neck as he talked. "And it's still raining. I hope you like mud, fella. You're going to be running fetlock deep in it today!"

Exterminator turned his head and grabbed the sleeve of McDaniel's jacket, tugging at it playfully. McDaniel chuckled. "Can't you even be serious today? The most important day of your life, and you want to play!" Bones answered with a joyful snort and with a toss of the head.

People had been coming around to look at him all day. Important people who hadn't bothered with him before. They speculated, and walked around inspecting him from every angle. They talked about his size, his frame, his high withers, his long neck, his disposition. He hadn't had so much attention in years.

Then they would shake their heads, shrug, and go away. Bones would poke his nose happily against McDaniel. For somehow, in all this activity, he had sensed that today he was going to the post. Today the bugle would blow for him.

Exterminator turned to look, as McDaniel did, at the sound of a strange voice.

"Howdy, sir. I'm Mike Terry, up from Virginia."

He was a stableboy, McDaniel guessed at a glance. His clothes were oddly assorted but clean. His dark hair was carefully combed. He had the tanned, healthy look of a youngster who was in the wind and sun a great deal. And his bright eyes, looking straight at McDaniel, were eager and honest.

"Howdy, Mike. Somebody send you to me?"

"Yes sir." The boy held out a pass. "I been working for Mr. Billy Garth—he trained me. He told me to look for you. Said he'd be obliged if you would fix it so's I can see the race."

Before he had finished his speech, the boy had turned from the trainer to the horse. His eyes moved expertly over the frame of the animal. He said, "Sure is a big fellow. Sure has a good strong frame. Is he the work horse they've been talking about taking Sun Briar's place?"

"Yes. This is Exterminator."

The boy grinned. He moved closer to Exterminator. "Man alive! He looks good to me." Mike put a gentle hand on the animal's head. "Say! Look at them eyes!

33

He's got hazel color in his eyes. Always been told hazel eyes are the mark of a champion!" He chuckled, delighted. "Yea, Bo! I think he's going to win. I swear, I think he's going to beat out all the others!"

McDaniel laughed. "Well, boy, that makes two of us. You and me. Just two of us. You get along now. Find yourself a place by the rail. If anybody questions you, tell them you work for me. I'll see you after the race."

The grandstands were beginning to fill. A roof of umbrellas covered the slow-moving lines that stretched to the admission windows. People surged around the men who were calling, "Programs, programs, get your programs!"

In the stables tension was mounting. The men felt it—grooms, trainers, exercise boys, everybody. They tried to be calm. But questions came sharply, answers were short, voices were edgy. The thoroughbreds felt it. They were restless in their stalls, atremble at sounds, shy at movements.

All but Bones. He watched the activity with interest and contentment.

A groom passing by said to McDaniel, "You know, Boss, I think Bones knows he's going to race today. Acts like he's pure happy about everything."

"Of course he knows."

McDaniel looked sharply at Bones.

"You know, all right. But do you know how tough it's going to be? Not just the mud. . . . But the crowd. They won't be with you. No, sir! Most of them won't even know you're in the race. You won't hear them calling your name, urging you on, cheering you to win. Not this time, old boy. Even your jockey is disappointed—

riding the work horse instead of Sun Briar. Oh, he'll give you a good ride, Willie Knapp will. He's an honest jockey and one of the best, but—" Bones rubbed his head against McDaniel's shoulder, and the trainer smiled. "You trying to tell me you don't mind? Well, I hope you don't. And I wish I didn't mind. I'd sure like to be as calm about it all as you are."

McDaniel glanced at his watch. It was almost time to saddle up. Ordinarily he would have honored a friend by inviting him to saddle the Derby entry. But he wasn't sure anybody would consider it an honor to saddle Old Bones. He would saddle Exterminator himself.

He called a groom.

He put a gentle hand on Old Bones' head and looked into the great, intelligent eyes. And he saw the hazel color, too. "There'll be a boy along the fence, calling your name. Listen to him. And listen to me. I'll be there talking to you, too. And win! Hear me? Run as you've never run before! Win!"

6 "RUN FOR THE ROSES!"

The horses were led out to the saddling paddock.

The rain had stopped. The day was still gray, but the sweetness of springtime was all about, and trees and lawns were a bright, new-washed green.

In the paddock the horses were led around and around the walking ring as they waited for the jockeys to be weighed in.

People pushed and shoved to get close to the fence that surrounded the paddock, fighting for a glimpse of the horses, hoping to be able to choose the one that would go down in racing history as the Derby winner.

McDaniel ignored the gibes people were making at Bones.

"Now, ain't that some horse? Look at him! . . . Kilmer must be out of his mind to let that sack full of bones carry his colors. . . . Heard Kilmer was running a work horse! He's a work horse for sure!"

The jockeys came into the paddock—small, neat figures in their bright silks. Willie Knapp, clad in the green, orange, and brown silks of the Kilmer stables, came over to Exterminator. McDaniel gave him a leg up.

Nobody saw Exterminator tremble with excitement

when the jockey's light weight touched his back. Nobody saw his quivering when the bugle sounded. Only Exterminator knew the excitement was there. And he stood waiting, very quietly.

Willie Knapp bent to adjust his stirrups, and a man yelled, "Hey, Knapp. Why don't you get a *horse?*" The crowd hooted, and Willie Knapp's face turned a deep red. Poor Willie. He had looked forward to riding Sun Briar, to winning the Derby. . . . But now!

McDaniel put a gentle hand on the horse's muzzle, and Exterminator nuzzled the hand. McDaniel spoke to him softly. "Remember what I told you, fella. You can do it." Then he smiled confidently at the jockey and said, "Hurry home, Willie. You're on the best horse, even if a lot of people don't think so."

Willie raised his crop in answer and took his place in the parade that wound up a ramp toward the track.

It was a bright parade, led by a scarlet-coated outrider on a gray pony.

The great crowd that watched was the largest that had ever seen a Kentucky Derby. People crowded into every inch of space in the clubhouse and the grandstands. And for a quarter of a mile a solid mass of people lined the lawns.

All heads turned in the direction of the approaching parade. All eyes strained to see the horses. Here they came—the thoroughbreds, prancing nervously, heads reared high. All except one. Bones sloshed along, his big head thrust forward on his long neck, as unconcerned as if he were hauling a load of hay. That's how he looked to those watching. They couldn't see the joy that filled the big bony body, joy that had been building up since midmorning, when he had known he would race that day.

The American flag was run up, fluttering bright against the sunless sky. The band began to play.

The crowds rose, and for a few solemn moments there was only the sound of the music, and all eyes were on the flag.

But the solemn moment ended, and the band music, if anything, had heightened the emotions, sharpened the excitement of the crowd.

Again everyone was watching the horses. Excitedly people called the name of the horse they hoped to see win as it passed by.

It was not difficult to see who the favorites were.

"Escoba! There he is—Escoba!" Ripples of cheers greeted Escoba.

"Hey, Sewell Combs!"

"War Cloud! War Cloud!" The stands broke into a noisy demonstration as the top favorite came by.

Not until the parade was far down the stretch on the way to the post was Exterminator's name called. There, crowded against the fence, Mike Terry watched. "You show 'em, Exterminator!" he shouted as the chestnut horse plodded by. A great roar of laughter exploded around him.

"Who's he gonna exterminate—himself?" a man yelled.

Mike looked straight ahead, his eyes on his horse, ignoring the laughter and the jokes that followed. He didn't care. Exterminator had heard him. Mike was sure he had seen him turn his head when his name was called.

Now the horses were at the post. The starters were

lining them up.

Nervously the thoroughbreds danced about, reared, and side-stepped. All but Bones. He stood where he had been put, looking unconcerned, paying not the slightest attention to the excited animals around him.

"Look at Exterminator. I swear he's asleep. . . . Look at the work horse, will you? Stuck in the mud he is. He'll never know when the race starts."

Kilmer pulled his hat down over his eyes. The sympathetic glances from his friends were almost worse than the biting comments. It would have been a different day, indeed, with Sun Briar in there! But that work horse! *What* had McDaniel got him into?

"THEY'RE OFF!" The words roared from the stands as the horses broke.

Kilmer looked to see how long his entry would stand at the post. *But he wasn't at the post!* Someone next to Kilmer was shouting, "Exterminator is fifth! Viva America broke on top—Escoba and American Eagle close behind. Sewell Combs next—yes, yes, Exterminator is fifth! At least he is *in* the race."

Kilmer rocked his chair so far forward it tipped, pitching him on the floor of the box. He picked himself up fast and trained his glasses on the moving line of horses. Where, where were those green, orange, and brown silks now?

The jockey, Willie Knapp, flattened himself against the powerful horse's neck and tried to see through the showering mud. Mud bombarded horse and rider from all sides. In front, a thundering wall of horses blocked them. Horses pounded close and threatening behind.

Willie looked desperately for a break in the solid mass

40

in front of him. He talked to Exterminator almost as if he were praying. "Please—we gotta get through, get through, get through. . . ."

Oh, Exterminator knew as well as Willie Knapp did. Old Bones, too, was looking for a little hole in that solid wall, a little space.

In spite of everything, the powerful, steady strides never broke their rhythm. He had to get through. . . . He moved toward the r   was a bold move. For jockeys whose horses w   tter positions were battling for the rail, too. It was a dangerous move. The rail, and tons of plunging, fighting horses. . . . But if he could find the little space. . . . A horse moved, and he saw the little space, so narrow. . . . It widened a bit, a little more. Should he try? It was now or never—Old Bones and jockey were hurtling through!

How could they see in mud like this? But horse and rider knew when they passed the others—Sewell Combs first, then American Eagle, then Escoba. Viva America was still in front, pelting them with mud.

McDaniel was watching, white and silent, and he saw and whispered, "Now, Bones. . . . Let him go Willie—go-go-go—"

Willie Knapp made a movement with his arm as if he had heard McDaniel. And Bones, understanding, poured more strength into his powerful strides.

Suddenly, amazingly, no mud rained in their faces. Bones and Willie knew they were in the lead.

But now another horse bore down on them. Close, too close—a nose, a head edged by them. It was Escoba! Escoba wanted it, too.

Escoba passed them, Willie crying, "No! No! No!" Bones agreed.

More power, more strength—Bones pulled even with Escoba. For a few seconds they ran neck and neck. Then the steady rhythmic strides sped faster, faster, and Bones pulled past Escoba—ahead by a neck, half a length, a full length! Bones was across the finish line!

A few seconds before, the stands had been filled with jumping, screaming people. Now the thousands stood paralyzed, silent. What had happened? Who was this horse? The stunned silence lasted only for seconds.

Then, wave on wave, the cheers came for the unknown, the work horse that had run so magnificent a race.

Old Bones, with Willie still in the saddle, stood in the winner's circle. Photographers and newsmen were waiting. Henry McDaniel came, limp-tired but happy. Bones saw him and turned his head toward him ever so slightly.

For a second McDaniel thought the horse was going to grab his sleeve playfully. But no. Bones realized the significance and import of the occasion. He merely looked at his trainer and gave him a slow wink, as if to say, "We fooled them, didn't we? We made it."

McDaniel acknowledged the wink with a quick nod.

Mr. Kilmer was there, being politely congratulated by people who were still shocked by the surprise finish.

The governor of the state was there, saying proud things about the Kentucky-bred Derby winner.

The huge horseshoe of red roses was lifted and hung around Old Bones' neck. He stood with dignity while the roses were put in place, while cameras clicked and people cheered, while reporters interviewed Kilmer, McDaniel, Willie Knapp.

Someone said, "He's the one horse nobody thought would wear those roses."

Henry McDaniel smiled. Nobody? There were two exceptions. McDaniel was one. The other was the boy, Mike Terry, who at that moment was down at the stable, waiting and hoping to be hired by Henry McDaniel.

Now Exterminator was led triumphantly back to the barn, where he was greeted by grooms, stablemen, and exercise boys. Now there were plenty of men eager to clean off the mud, sponge him, rub him down, cool him out. He whinnied happily. Never before had he had so much affectionate attention.

"Good Old Bones—look at him, calm as if he'd taken a run down the pike! Hey, Exterminator! How you like those roses, boy? Jumping Jupiter! Never saw anything like it in all my born days!"

Shouts of joy went up when word came to the barn that Mr. Kilmer was doubling everybody's salary for the month of May. "Good Old Bones!" the men cried. "Hurray for Exterminator! Hear that old fellow? Double dough—thanks to you!"

Through all the excitement a boy stood back, watch-

ing, waiting. One of the grooms yelled, "Hey, boy! Who are you?"

McDaniel came into the barn just in time to hear the question. His voice thundered, and everyone listened, for Henry McDaniel was usually a quiet-spoken man.

"Who is he? I'll tell you. He's our newest hand, hired today. He's Mike Terry. He's the only one of the lot of you who believed Exterminator would win! That's who he is!"

Everyone was quiet for a second. Then Henry McDaniel broke into a big grin and shouted, "Come on over here, Mike, and meet the rest of the clan."

Exterminator was back in his stall, munching contentedly on hay. The barn was quiet. All who could get away had gone into Louisville to celebrate.

Henry McDaniel went back to have one more look

at Bones before leaving. He found Mike there, stroking the horse's head, talking to him softly.

"You love horses, don't you, boy?" At the voice Mike turned in surprise.

"Yes, sir, I do. Especially this one. I knew the minute I laid eyes on him, he was the horse I'd been looking for all my life."

"Seems like he's real fond of you, too," Henry McDaniel said, watching Bones nuzzle the boy with his soft nose.

Mike smiled. "I reckon he knows how I feel about him—I think he understands."

"I think so too, Mike. And I think you'll make a fine team." He smiled. "Did the boys fix you up with a room?"

"Yes, sir. And if the food tonight was a sample, I'd say you feed real good here at the Kilmer stables."

"Tonight might have been a bit special. But I never hear any complaints." Henry McDaniel turned to go. "I'm going to count on you to take good care of Exterminator, Mike."

"Oh, I will," the boy said. "I will." His face was shining with happiness. "I will never leave him, as long as he lives."

And Mike Terry never did.

7 THE GALLOPING
HATRACK

The exhilaration of the race was still with Old Bones. He woke every morning at daybreak, eager for the barn door to be opened and the day to begin. He was no longer a work horse. Again, now, he was being exercised and trained for racing.

In the barn, in the paddocks, at the track, arguments boiled around him.

Some people said, "His winning the Derby was a fluke. Exterminator can't run. You'll see—he'll never win another big race."

Others said, "Maybe he can run in mud. But how will he do on a clear day with a fast track? How will he do in shorter races? His winning the Derby doesn't mean a thing."

Even Mr. Kilmer—happy though he was to have won the Derby—did not seem to think highly of Old Bones as a race horse. For, when a reporter asked, "You really bought Exterminator with the idea of racing him in the Derby, didn't you?" Mr. Kilmer answered hotly, "I did not. When I acquired him I didn't even know he was eligible for the Derby. Exterminator was bought purely as a work horse. As a race horse I still don't consider him in the same class with Sun Briar."

When Mike heard this, he said, "Course you're not in the same class! You're in a class all by yourself—and it's the top class, it is."

Shortly after the Derby, Henry McDaniel, watching Mike rubbing down Bones, said, "How would you two like to go to New York?"

Mike's bright, dark eyes flashed like light bulbs at Henry McDaniel.

"You mean to Belmont?"

"Yes. We're entering Bones in the Turf and Field Handicap at Belmont on May twenty-fifth."

Mike let out a whoop and a holler. "Belmont, here we come! We'll show you all what speed *is!*"

Bones, hearing the happy voice, whinnied loudly and snatched Mike's sleeve.

McDaniel grinned at the pair. "I suppose you'll travel by boxcar, Mike?"

"Yessirreeee! I'll ride right in the boxcar with Bones, and I won't take my eyes off him the whole trip through." Suddenly Mike was serious. "That's a long trip. Suppose he's not a good shipper? Suppose he won't eat?"

"That we will have to find out, Mike. But I wouldn't worry. Old Bones is calm about everything else—I expect he'll be a good shipper."

There were other horses taking the long ride from Kentucky to New York. Mike had watched them being loaded—rearing, side-stepping, shying away. He heard them stomping in the cars, nickering nervously.

His eyes were anxious on Bones. Bones gave him a long, straight look; then went into the boxcar as unconcerned as if he were being led into his barn stall. He

EXTERMINAT
(OLD BO

had been shipped by boxcar before. He knew that as soon as you got used to the movement, to the clickety-click, clickety-clack sound of the train, it was fine.

He looked around. There was a rack of fresh hay. There was clean straw on the floor. There was fresh water to drink. All the things he needed. He took a mouthful of hay and chewed it slowly. He took a long drink of water. Then he lay down on the straw in the car and went to sleep.

When they reached New York, Mike bragged to Mr. McDaniel, "Relaxed as a hound dog, he was. Ate the whole way, same as at home. Look at him—you'd never know he'd left his own stall."

"He looks fine. I thought he'd be a good shipper." Mr. McDaniel patted Bones' shoulder. "How do you like New York, old fella?"

Bones nuzzled his trainer with his big, soft nose and whinnied happily.

"He likes it fine," Mike said, "and wait till he wins that big race—he'll like it even better."

Mike told everybody who would listen how Exterminator was going to walk away with the race. Sometimes exercise boys and grooms teased Mike. "You trying to tell me that big loose-jointed thing can run? Sure he won the Derby—so what?" And the arguments would begin. But Mike refused to listen. Nothing could shake his confidence. He knew.

In the paddock before the race, Mike grinned at the comments he heard from the crowd. "So that's Exterminator! Homely, isn't he? . . . Big, bony fellow. . . . May have won the Derby, but he won't take this one! . . . Doesn't look like much of a race horse to me. . . ."

To himself Mike said, "Just wait till the race is over, people. You'll change your tune."

Hanging on the fence, his eyes glued on the horses, Mike wasn't worried when Exterminator stayed behind for the first few furlongs. He'd move when he wanted to. And he did.

Mike saw him pull away from the field, move into third place, then second place. Mike began to yell. Who was that horse in the lead? The crowd was yelling, "It's

Kilts II. It's Kilts. . . ." Horrified, unbelieving, Mike saw Kilts II go over the finish line ahead of Exterminator.

He stood limp, trembling, while Kilts II was led to the winner's circle. He saw Exterminator—his head down, every line of his body showing dejection—walk slowly back to the barn.

"Poor old Bones," Mike said to him while he was being rubbed down and cooled out. "You know you lost, don't you? Look at him, Mr. McDaniel; he knows."

"I believe he does," Henry McDaniel agreed. For there were no joyful whinnies or playful nips now. With his head slumped down, his eyes half closed, Exterminator was truly a sad-looking animal.

"What happened?" Mike begged for an answer.

"Nothing happened. He ran second." Henry McDaniel tried to keep the disappointment out of his voice. "Is that so bad? Stop looking as if it were the end of the world, Mike." And to Exterminator, "You can't win all the time, old fella. And you ran a good race. Cheer up now—wait till next time. Wait till we get you up to Saratoga."

"Are we going to Saratoga?" Mike asked.

"Sure thing." Henry McDaniel spun a silver dollar toward Mike, saying, "Catch. . . . Now, go get yourself a square meal and stop mourning."

In the boxcar with Exterminator, on the way to Saratoga, Mike's hopes were high as the stars.

Poor Mike! He would have been in the depths of despair had he known the bitter truth: Exterminator was not to win a single race that summer.

At Saratoga he lost his first race, then another, and another.

Each race, for Old Bones, started with that wonderful

surge of excitement, a sense of power and strength, the feeling that he could outrun any animal alive and never tire. Oh, this time surely he would romp easily home, lengths ahead of all the others.

But something would happen! He wouldn't quite make it. Across the finish line—but always with one, maybe two, others ahead of him, throwing dust in his eyes, kicking dirt in his face. And the wonderful exhilaration of the race was spoiled. He had not won.

Mike was inconsolable. He pretended not to be when the others boys, the grooms and stable hands, teased him. He said, "Never mind! Give Exterminator time. Hecktalooie! The Derby was only the fifth race he ran in his whole life. Wait till he has a little more experience. He'll leave your nag so far behind you won't know he's in the race. You'll see!"

But to Henry McDaniel he moaned, "What's wrong?"

"Nothing is wrong, Mike. He's racing well and training well."

"I think it's the rides the jockeys are giving him." Mike shook his head. "If they'd let him run the race his own way, he'd win. He's different from other horses. He's smarter. They shouldn't try to tell him what to do. Maybe the jockeys have to learn how to ride him. . . ."

McDaniel put his hand on the boy's shoulder. "You may be right, Mike. But stop eating your heart out. Wait until fall."

"Fall!" Mike groaned. Watching the hot August sun that boiled through the barn door, the boy felt that fall was a long time off. A long time to wait.

But it came, of course. And there was Mike, hanging on to the fence for that first fall race, confident, but a little anxious, too, silently saying, "You'll win —you've *got* to win—you'll win. . . ."

Then the yells as Exterminator took the lead, the excited screaming as he held it and made winning look easy.

Mike was almost bursting with happiness as he watched Exterminator step proudly, head high, to the winner's circle. Old Bones felt good, too!

Oh, that fall was well worth waiting for!

Now Exterminator ran as he loved to, as he had wanted to before—freely, joyously, nothing holding him back, nothing passing him, either!

One race after another he won, and the crowds roared, "Look at that galloping hatrack run! Look at that wonderful old skin full of bones romp home . . . ! It's Exterminator again. . . . Sure, it's Exterminator . . . !"

He won them easily, almost effortlessly. And it seemed to Bones, when the jockey pulled him up and walked him to the winner's circle, that he could have run on and on.

Looking at him, Mike would brag. "He's breathing as lightly as if he hadn't been running. Isn't that something? You wouldn't know he'd been in a race."

Thanksgiving that year was the happiest one Mike had ever known. On that day Bones won the Thanksgiving Handicap at Latonia. It was the sixth race he had won in the fall meet. And now there were few doubters watching Exterminator run.

Mike had all the turkey he could eat, with all the trimmings. And Exterminator had three of the biggest, shiniest apples Mike could find.

There was frost in the air, and racing was over until early spring. Bones looked thin after his racing. Mr. McDaniel said to Mike, "We're going to take him down to Hot Springs, Arkansas, for the winter and put a little meat on those bones. He'll be a four-year-old when spring racing starts, so he'll be eligible next year for some big races. We want to have him ready."

Actually Exterminator would not have his fourth birthday until the thirtieth of May. But all thoroughbreds have their official birthday on the same day: the first of January. Even if a foal is born on the thirty-first of December, he is officially one year old on New Year's Day.

This birthday rule was made long ago by the Jockey Club. It has a sound reason behind it. In many races only horses of a certain age are allowed to run. In the Kentucky Derby, for example, only three-year-olds can run. There are other races in which all horses must be three years old or older, or two years old, or four years old.

Before all thoroughbreds were given an official birthday on January 1st, there was a great deal of confusion. A horse might run in a race for two-year-olds one week, have his third birthday the next day, and compete in a race for three-year-olds the next week. It was impossible to keep track of the true ages of all horses, with birthdays scattered throughout the year.

Friends often celebrate the real birthday of a thoroughbred. Exterminator's birthday was always remembered on the thirtieth of May. But his official age, like that of all thoroughbreds, was dated from the first of January in the year in which he was born.

On his third official birthday, Exterminator was unknown.

Now, a year later, his name was familiar to millions, and hundreds of thousands had watched him race. People were asking, "What kind of a record will he make as a four-year-old?"

In Arkansas a man, a boy, and a horse were doing their best to make sure that record would be a good one.

8   FRIENDS, FAME
AND FORTUNE

When training for spring racing began, Mr. McDaniel
let Mike Terry exercise Bones.

Mike took this responsibility very seriously. He knew
that an able exercise boy is extremely important to a
race horse. The boy must have good hands, and a knack
for handling a horse surely but gently. He must understand what the trainer wants and follow directions
carefully. He must have an almost superhuman sense
of timing and judgment of pace so that when he breezes
his horse—lets him go fast as he wants—the boy can tell
to the fraction of a second how fast his horse has run.

Most important of all, he must have a kind of intu-
ition for how his horse feels and behaves, and a quick
understanding if anything is even slightly wrong. No
wonder many horsemen believe good exercise boys are
harder to find than good jockeys!

Mike was proud to be Exterminator's exercise boy.
But he wanted to be more to him than that. An exercise
boy might spend only a short time each day with a
thoroughbred.

So Mike not only exercised him, he rubbed him down,
groomed him, watered him, fed him, talked to him, and

watched over him day and night.

Early in March Exterminator ran his first race as a four-year-old.

He won it.

After the race, Mr. McDaniel said, "You did fine, old fella. Now in three weeks you're going to have a chance to answer one of the questions the doubters are asking. Can you sprint? Everybody knows you're okay in a long race. But how about a sprint?"

"He can," Mike said stoutly. "They'll see. Won't they, Bones?"

McDaniel laughed. But his voice was serious when he said, "I hope you're right, Mike. But take it easy. Don't be too sure."

Mr. McDaniel knew that usually a horse that liked longer races could not sprint. Exterminator, as a rule, started out slowly, gradually came up, and won in a strong finish. If he ran like that in the sprint—which was only three quarters of a mile—the race would be over before Exterminator began to move up.

But he didn't run like that. Mike was right.

Exterminator broke at the start with the lightning speed he usually saved for the finish. Off like a shot, in the lead, across the finish line.

"It's Exterminator, Exterminator. . . ." The crowd went wild. Now they said, "He can win at any distance. . . . Usually starts slow. . . . How did he know that was a sprint and he had to be off in a burst of speed? How did he know?"

Mike winked at Exterminator. "He reads the program, that's how he knows. I take him a program before a race, and he looks to see what length the race

is. Don't you, Old Bones?" Mike laughed gleefully.

A reporter, watching the boy and the horse, said, "I can almost believe you, Son. Anyhow, one thing sure—distance doesn't bother him."

The truth was, nothing seemed to bother Exterminator. As spring went into summer and summer into fall, this fact amazed and delighted the crowds more and more.

The weather? It affected most thoroughbreds. They

didn't like mud, or they didn't like rain, or they did like mud, or they didn't like heat. Exterminator liked everything.

All he required was a track to run on, horses to race with, an excited crowd watching from the grandstands, and he was happy.

It was fine, of course, to have a pleasantly cool day and a fast, dry track. But it was just as much of a race when he was kicking through mud, or when the rain fell hard, like a thousand little silver whips urging him on faster, faster. On a day like that, too, the sponge and rubdown after the race felt good. Good, too, the snugness of the barn, with Mike talking to him and plenty of fresh hay to chew on. He liked the rain.

He liked the heat, too. He never felt like complaining on a hot, sultry day as others did. For one thing, that kind of weather brought the crowds out. And he loved a big crowd roaring, the swarms of people before the race, pressing against the paddock fence. Often he saw somebody he knew. Sometimes even Mike didn't understand whom he was whinnying at and stretching his long head toward. Like the day he spotted that lady in the crowd—a lady who had brought him apples on his birthday. Mike didn't remember her. But Exterminator did. And was she surprised! Exterminator wouldn't join the parade to the post until she had come over to the fence and greeted him.

Yes, summer weather certainly brought out the crowds. And for him, a hot day spoiled none of the joy of racing.

When it grew cold in the fall, toward the end of November, he liked the bite of the wind in his face, the track frosty-hard beneath his flying hooves. Then the barn felt good, too—warm, and friendly with the sound of men's voices, for it was too chilly to dawdle out of doors.

No, the weather never worried him. To Old Bones, all weather was racing weather.

Then, there was the matter of tracks. Some thoroughbreds were fussy about where they raced. This, Exterminator could never understand. Whether a track was in the North, East, South, or West, it was still a track, built to be run on. As such, it was a joy to behold, and wherever it was, it felt wonderfully good under his hooves. He was always glad to be back on it.

As a four-year-old, Exterminator did more than make a brilliant record. He made thousands and thousands of friends, all over the country.

His last race that fall was the Pimlico Cup. And he won it. It should have been a happy time for all.

But over the stable hung a cloud of sadness. Old Bones and his friend, Henry McDaniel were saying good-by to each other. McDaniel was leaving as trainer for Mr. Kilmer and going to work for another stable.

In spite of Bones' victory, it was a black day for Mike, too.

McDaniel saw the question in Mike's eyes. He said, "I know you wonder why I'm leaving—how I can leave Old Bones. Well, leaving him is hard, believe me. But you know, Mike, in this business we trainers always seem to move around. Maybe it's that farther fields look greener. More likely it's that another stable owner gets us excited over his crop of promising two-year-olds, over the colts he owns that would win everything in sight *if* they had the right trainer—and we see a new challenge, greater opportunity. So, we break the ties—mighty close ties some of them are, too," he said, looking from Mike to Exterminator, "and we go. . . ." They stood quietly, the three of them. Then Henry McDaniel said, "You could come with me, Mike. But you won't, will you?"

Mike shook his head. "No. I'll never leave Old Bones." His voice was husky. "Some folks are already saying he won't run as well with another trainer."

Henry McDaniel put his hand on Exterminator's head. "That's nonsense! Isn't it, old fella? You'll go right on racing and winning and loving it, you will." He rubbed the white spots between Bones' eyes and stroked the big, beautiful head. "We'll meet from time to time, here and there. Yes, sir. I'll be seeing you. Don't forget me."

He shook hands with Mike and said, "Good luck, Mike boy. Take good care of Old Bones. He's the only one of his kind." Then he turned and walked away.

Bones whinnied softly, as if to call him back. But his friend was gone.

Mike put an arm across the big horse's shoulders. The horse lowered his head and nuzzled the boy gently. Thus each comforted the other for his loss.

When the new trainer came, Bones and Mike greeted him courteously and did as they were told. They liked him. They did not love him as they had Mr. McDaniel. But he was a man they respected.

In the spring, Exterminator raced as brilliantly as he had under Henry McDaniel's training.

Soon, however, the new trainer left. Another came

to take his place. That trainer left, and another came.

For various reasons, there was a procession of trainers for Exterminator.

Having so many different handlers would have been ruinous for most race horses. They could not have taken the constant change of personalities, of techniques and methods.

But Old Bones liked and respected each man. A new trainer was also a new friend. He raced well for all of them. Some of them he made famous.

9   A GALLANT FINISH

When people said nothing bothered Old Bones, they were wrong.

One thing bothered him a lot. That was the bad actor whose behavior held up the start of a race, the temperamental thoroughbred who pitched, reared and shied at the post when all the other horses were lined up, ready to go.

When Old Bones was racing there were no mechanical starting gates as there are today. A wire or tape was stretched across the track at the post. At a signal from the starter it was raised—and the horses were off. But before the signal was given, all horses had to be standing ready, in position, so the start would be fair. When an animal behaved badly, assistant starters tried to hold him in check, coax him into position, calm him down. Often the antics of one horse excited others, and the men had a real melee on their hands. It was ticklish work, and dangerous.

Old Bones didn't look bothered. He always stood calmly, almost wearily, waiting for the temper tantrum to calm down.

Nobody knew it bothered him—until the day he decided to do something about it.

The horses were at the post. Then a nervous colt began acting up—side-stepping, rearing up, snorting and dancing.

The crowds in the grandstands watched tensely, binocular and field glasses trained on the horses. Suddenly, excitedly, people began to cry out, "Look! Something's wrong with Exterminator! . . . What's going on? Something's wrong—" But then the starter signaled, and the horses were off. Exterminator soon took the lead, held it handsomely, and crossed the finish line first. But even as they cheered him, people were asking, "What happened? Exterminator was leaning over. He looked as if he was going to collapse. What went on?"

It was the starter who explained it.

"Good Old Bones got disgusted and took steps, that's all. Went over to that fractious colt and leaned against him. Meantime, I reckon, talked some horse sense into him. Anyhow, the colt calmed down, and they were off." The starter laughed. "Sure glad I had plenty of witnesses. Otherwise folks would accuse me of telling a tall tale. Most amazing thing I ever saw—and something, very likely, we will never see again."

But the starter was wrong. Bones had learned how to cope with the one thing that bothered him. Now he didn't wait until the temperamental one got completely out of control. He went into action as soon as the fuss began.

One starter said, "Old Bones should be paid a salary as an assistant starter at these tracks." Other starters, and their assistants, agreed.

No wonder people came to the races now especially to see Old Bones. He always put on a good show.

In the paddock, as the horses were ready to parade to the track, he waited for the question, and the question always came. "Hey, Old Bones," somebody was sure to yell, "are you winning this one?" Bones would look in the direction of the question, his wise eyes on the crowd. Slowly he blinked his eyes in a kind of wink that seemed to say, "Yes, friend, I am. It's in the bag." And the crowd would cheer.

He had his own style of winning a race, too. He almost never won by a large margin, though often he could have. But he slowed down after taking the lead, and won by a head. Or, if he came from behind, he merely nosed the leader out. It made the other horses look better, didn't it?

The horse coming in second was not humiliated by being left way behind. It made a more exciting race, too. The cheering grandstands were proof of that. It was a good way to win a race. It was Old Bones' way. And the crowds loved it.

Having won, he knew, too, what the crowds waited for. Nobody left the grandstands until he came by, head high, stepping proudly. The spectators roared; they screamed his name. He always acknowledged the ovation with a deep nod of his head, a kind of small bow of triumph.

Of course, he did not always win. When he lost he walked by slowly, his head lowered. Even when he lost, the people cheered him. But the sound did not gladden him then. He went miserably back to the barn to await Mike's comforting words, "You can't win *all* the time. You ran a good race." Then the lump of sugar or the crisp carrot or apple Mike slipped him to help brighten a dark moment.

As time went on, Old Bones and Mike became a well-traveled pair. It was fortunate that Bones was a good shipper and that Mike didn't mind going along.

From Virginia to Kentucky, north to Canada, down to Maryland, up to New York, out to Chicago, west to California, south into Mexico, back to Kentucky.

Wherever they went, Exterminator found old friends waiting for him. Mike would hear the high, joyful whinny and say, "Well, who is it now?"

Here would come a groom who had taken care of him in the past, a jockey who had ridden him, a stable hand, an exercise boy, an admirer of whom Old Bones was fond.

Mike would grin and say, "You never forget anybody, do you? You're more loyal than most people."

Once in a while the whinny would be especially joyful, and the great head would bob in excitement. Mike knew then it would be Mr. McDaniel for a brief but happy reunion.

As they traveled, the silver cups, the shining trophies Exterminator won at various places through the years were shipped back to the Kilmer farm in Virginia. There Mr. Kilmer had them proudly on display. No other horse in America had ever built up such a record as a winner of cup races.

Mr. Kilmer, long since, had admitted that Exterminator was a great race horse. He was very proud of him. But his belief in Sun Briar had been justified, too. Sun Briar had won his share of victories in his day, although he was retired while Exterminator was still winning races, still running strong.

As Old Bones won more and more races, proving himself superior to other horses, he was required to carry heavier and heavier weights when he raced. The heavy weights were supposed to handicap him and give the other horses a chance to win. At times he had to carry as much as thirty pounds more than some of the horses he was racing with.

When he had to race with the unheard-of amount of one hundred and forty pounds—or even more—many people were outraged. They said, "Don't forget, it was the last straw that broke the camel's back!"

Then one of his friends quipped:

There was a camel whose back was broke.
One more straw made the poor beast croak.
It's lucky Old Bones is a thoroughbred.
If he was a camel, he'd be dead.

While people laughed at the jingle, they still worried about the heavy weights. Mike worried, too. But Old Bones wasn't worried. He kept right on winning races, sending silver cups back to Virginia.

Exterminator felt the burden of those added weights. But he never objected to them.

To carry the extra weight across the finish line first often meant summoning up extra strength, more power, more courage. As he grew older and the weights grew heavier, it took more and more grit to pull together that extra strength when he needed it.

But he did. He had to. Why? Because the thunder of the other horses, the jockeys' cries, the roar from the grandstands, and his own heart told him he had to!

When he was nine years old, people said, "He's too old to race. Surely Mr. Kilmer will retire him now."

Mr. Kilmer looked him over. He said, "You're nine years old. And you grew a little fat over the winter." He watched him on the exercise track, and said, "You're still strong, though, and eager to run. You still love to race, don't you?"

Yes, Exterminator was still eager to go.

So, Mr. Kilmer decided to send him down to Mexico for two races that spring. But he had to get somebody to train him first and put him in top condition.

At his age, however, Old Bones' training would have to be done with care and affection. Who could do it?

Out in California Henry McDaniel heard of Mr. Kilmer's plan.

He said, "Let Mike bring Old Bones out here to me. I'll train him."

A few days later Mike and Old Bones began the long trip across the continent that was to end in a happy reunion.

The reunion was not a long one, but Bones and Mike and Mr. McDaniel all enjoyed it. When it was time for the Mexican races, Old Bones was in beautiful condition. He won his first race in Mexico. And even though he lost the second one, Mr. McDaniel was very proud of him. "Look at him," he said, beaming at Mike, "more than twice as old as some of the colts he's running against, and he can still outdistance them."

Then Mr. McDaniel said good-by to his friends again. Mike and Old Bones went back to the States, then on up to Canada.

In Montreal the crowds cheered wildly when Exterminator came romping in, well in the lead in his first race there. "Look at him run," they screamed. "Good Old Bones! Nine years old—and watch him run!"

A man yelled, "He'll be running like this when he's twelve years old, I'll wager."

"Twelve?" another said. "Make it fifteen!"

But they were wrong.

Two weeks later Bones was led to the paddock ready to run in the Queens Hotel Handicap. This was his hundredth race. He looked fit and happy as Mike Terry led him around the paddock.

"You gonna take this one, Old Bones?" an admirer yelled. Old Bones gave him the knowing look, the slow blink, that the crowd always waited for.

And at first he thought he was going to take it. He ran easily, happily, moving up when he wanted to from fifth to fourth place. Then something happened. One leg wasn't working properly. The wonderful rhythm of the running was broken. Pain, sharp and agonizing, gnawed at the leg. But Old Bones didn't stop. He threw more strength, more heart into the race—and now he was in third place. . . . The pain was like fire burning. Still he raced on, trying for the lead, trying to cross that finish line first! But the pain, the broken rhythm, held him back. He finished third.

Only then did the great crowd see Old Bones was so lame he could hardly walk.

Mike was crying helplessly, unashamed. Mr. Kilmer rushed from his box, horrified. He berated the jockey, "Why on earth did you keep him in the race? Surely you could tell he'd gone lame!"

The poor jockey said, "I could tell, sir. But I couldn't stop him. He was determined to finish—he was trying to win it."

Back in the barn Mike waited in anguish while the vet examined Old Bones' leg.

"Poor old fellow," the vet said. "He must have been

in terrible pain, running on that leg. But it's going to be all right. He may not race again, but he'll walk on it. And he won't be lame."

Sadly Mr. Kilmer announced that Exterminator, beloved Old Bones, would be retired to green pastures on the Kilmer farm in Virginia.

Those who watched his last race would never forget it. They did not see him win. But they saw one of the most gallant performances ever witnessed.

10 A PONY NAMED PEANUTS

At first Old Bones was fooled. He did not know he was retired. He thought he was resting up on the Virginia farm between races, as he had done before.

His leg was all right. Each morning Mike took him out and exercised him. Old Bones assumed he was being kept in condition for future racing. He did not know that Mike exercised him because a horse that has been racing cannot be put out to pasture at once. He must be slowed down by degrees.

Soon the morning gallops became less strenuous. Then the easy gallops were gradually slowed down to a canter. Bones was baffled. He had never been exercised like this before.

Other horses breezed past him, pounding down the stretch, and he was held back. Why wouldn't Mike let him go?

Suddenly he knew. The horses that breezed past him were training to return to the track! He was not going back to the track. They were slowing him down —and he would never race again.

Rebellion, such as he had never felt before, took

possession of him. He pawed the floor of his stall and kicked the wall. He threw himself against the doors and tried to batter them down. He filled the barn with his noise and fury.

Mike said, "Poor old fellow. Maybe you're stabled too close to the exercise track. Maybe if we put you in a barn farther away, where you can't hear the track noises, you'll be better."

So he was moved to another barn. But this made no difference in the way he felt or in the way he behaved.

He heard Mike's voice talking to him, but he would not listen. He saw other people come to stare at him, puzzled, shocked at his behavior, and they tried to talk to him, too. He did not hear them. He loved Mike; he had always loved people. But people weren't enough for him now. They did not fill the great emptiness or replace what he had lost. Always before he had taken everything—the good and the bad—quietly. But against this he must protest. He must protest loudly and with action.

Poor Mike understood. He suffered with Old Bones. Something had to be done. But what? The sad thing, the certain thing, was that they could not give him what he wanted. He could not be returned to the track.

Finally Mike went to Mr. Kilmer. He said, "Mr. Kilmer, maybe if we could get a little pony as a companion for Old Bones it would help. You see, sir, Old Bones was in love with racing. Now he's had to give that up, and we must find something to take its place. I believe part of his trouble is loneliness."

Mr. Kilmer said, "It's worth trying. Something must be done quickly. Buy a pony—get one right away."

It wasn't as easy as Mike thought to find a little pony. When one was found, Mike wasn't entirely satisfied, because he was quite old. But he was docile and affectionate and would show them, at least, if a companion was what Old Bones needed.

Brought into the paddock, the little old pony stood still, quietly watching the big horse. Old Bones walked over to the little fellow. The pony trembled. Old Bones put his head down and sniffed gently at the little pony, telling him not to be afraid. The pony sniffed back.

Bones walked off a little way and turned to see if the pony was following. He was. Old Bones whinnied and perked up his ears. He ran a short distance, and the pony ran to catch up.

There was no doubt about it — Old Bones had a friend.

He had always loved to play, and now for the first time in his life, he had a playmate. He nuzzled the pony and nipped at its ears.

The men watching laughed. Mike said, "Alongside Old Bones the pony is no bigger than a peanut." So

his name became Peanuts.

Old Bones was quiet now, and all his attention was centered on his new friend.

When night came, Mike put the pony in the stall with Old Bones. They lay down in the sweet straw, side by side, and went to sleep. Old Bones was no longer lonely.

There were few reminders of his racing days now. His life with Peanuts was pleasant and comfortable, and he was willing to accept it.

Nearby, in another barn, Sun Briar lived in retirement. He and Old Bones were so different temperamentally that they would never be great friends. However, from their neighboring paddocks they called to each other now and again. But Old Bones asked for no four-legged companionship other than Peanuts'.

People he still loved. Visitors came to see Old Bones, bringing apples and carrots and cubes of sugar. Mike Terry rubbed him down, sponged him, combed and brushed him, watched over him lovingly and anticipated his every wish and need.

Mike would say, "You worked hard and raced well, old boy. Now enjoy your leisure."

As time went on, Mike's only real worry was Peanuts. The poor old fellow was getting very feeble. He tried to follow Old Bones about and keep him company. But more and more he found it necessary to lie down and rest.

He had been Old Bones' companion for three years now, and the pair were inseparable.

One afternoon Peanuts lay down in his stall and did not want to get up.

The vet came and said to Mike, "Poor old man! He's lived a long, long life, and a happy one. But I'm afraid he's too old to last much longer. We'd better move him out of the stall—Exterminator might hurt him."

Mike said, "Oh, no. Exterminator wouldn't hurt Peanuts for the world! And I don't think he would let us take Peanuts out of the stall."

Off and on through that night Mike came in. The pony lay stiffly on the straw, scarcely breathing. Old Bones stayed quiet in the corner, watching, waiting.

When Mike came in at dawn, the little pony had breathed his last. Poor Old Bones had finally fallen

asleep—his beautiful head resting gently on the pony's stiff little flank.

Stablemen came to take the pony's little body from the stall. Old Bones snorted angrily at them. He did not want them to touch his friend. He knew something was wrong. He did not understand what it was. But he would not allow anyone to touch Peanuts.

The men tried again. Never before had he wanted to hurt men. But now he had to fight for Peanuts. He lashed out at the men, kicking and stomping. But he was careful not to step on the pony.

Mike set food and water down for him. But he would not eat. He would not drink. All day he stood guard over the body of the pony.

Mike said to Mr. Kilmer, "I'll have to get a shank on Exterminator's halter and lead him out of the stall, into the stable yard. That's the only way we can get the pony out of the stall."

This Mike managed to do. But nothing Mike said could quiet him. He led Old Bones out, rearing and pitching, wild and unmanageable.

Everyone was frantic.

Mr. Kilmer said, "We must get another pony—right away! It won't be his old friend, but at least it might appease him, quiet him, to have a new companion. Certainly no *man*—not even Mike—can do anything with him."

Where could they find a pony on such short notice?

One of the men remembered friends of the Kilmers' who had a little pony. But they lived more than two hundred miles away. Even if they would give their pony up, it would take quite a while to get it to the Kilmer farm.

Meantime Mike Terry and various stablemen were taking turns holding Old Bones as well as they could, while he continued to act like a beast gone mad.

Mr. Kilmer called his friends long-distance. Yes, if it was for Old Bones they would bring their pony. Yes, they would hurry.

At two o'clock in the morning a pickup truck drove into the stable yard. Old Bones was still wild with grief, and it was all the men could do, two at a time, to hold him.

The truck was backed up to the loading stand, and the pony led down the ramp.

Exterminator bolted toward the pony, almost knocking down the two grooms who had been trying to control him. For a minute the men watching were afraid he would hurt the tiny stranger.

But the pony wasn't scared. He stood wide-eyed, curious, watching.

Old Bones rushed to him, sniffed him, rubbed him gently with his big, soft noze, nuzzled him with his head. He whinnied softly to the little pony, and the little pony answered.

Bones knew, of course, that this wasn't his old friend. But it was a new friend, a friend he needed desperately and one he would love.

He waited, making sure his new friend was going into the barn with him. Then he let Mike lead him into his stall.

Exhausted, he stretched out on the straw beside the tiny Shetland and fell asleep.

It had been a long, hard day for all.

11 THE
BIRTHDAY PARTY

The little new pony was beautiful. His coat was a rich chestnut. He had a silvery white mane and tail and a bright white blaze down the middle of his face. He was very tiny, just thirty-two inches high.

Mike Terry said, "We'll call him Peanuts, too." So he was named Peanuts II.

Old Bones had a fine playmate now.

They ran and romped together until little Peanuts was breathless. On nice days they played in the sunshine, rolled in the grass, and stretched out in the shade of the big old trees if the sun was hot. When the weather was bad, they could exercise in a fine walking ring in the barn. Their stall was large and comfortable. Their food was the best, and there was always plenty of fresh, sweet hay to nibble on between meals.

Old Bones found he could tease Peanuts. He would nip at his silver mane, holding on so the little pony had to stand still or get his hair pulled. Then Old Bones would let go, and race off, the pony following.

Sometimes he would playfully crowd Peanuts into a fence corner, gently leaning toward him so that the pony was trapped. When Peanuts squealed, as if to

say, "I've had enough. Stop it!" Old Bones would be off with a snort, Peanuts after him.

Peanuts learned to tease back. He nipped at Old Bones' legs, like a puppy. Sometimes, standing beside his big friend, the pony would walk right under Old Bones' belly and surprise him by appearing suddenly on the other side.

When they tired of games and play, they would just visit. "Talking to each other," Mike Terry would say. "Look at Old Bones. He's telling Peanuts all about his great days of the past."

At night they were cozy and comfortable together in the big stall.

Not for one minute would Old Bones allow the pony

to be separated from him. Even when Mike led them in or out of the barn, Old Bones insisted they be led together. Peanuts returned this devotion. He wanted to be close to his friend all the time.

The days were never dull. Many people came to visit Old Bones. For though his racing days were long since over, he was still very famous.

Some of his visitors were old friends. Henry McDaniel came whenever he was anywhere nearby. Willie Knapp, his old jockey; Mr. Milam, who had bought him as a yearling; and Mrs. Milam, who had given him his name. There were many others—starters he had helped, newspaper reporters who had written stories about him, sports writers who had covered his races, jockeys and trainers he had worked with, and won with.

When old friends gathered, there was always reminiscing.

"What was Exterminator's greatest race, Mike—not counting the Derby?"

"That would be hard to name, wouldn't it, Old Bones?" Mike answered. "He ran a lot of great ones. I reckon I was never more pleased, though, than when he won the Autumn Gold Cup at Belmont as a five-year-old."

"Tell it, Mike."

"Well, a rumor started early in the day that Exterminator wasn't in condition. And it spread like wildfire. He had to carry a lot of weight in that race, and the race was a long one—two miles.

"I knew he was in condition. I said to him, 'Bones boy, you go out there and prove that what those folks are saying isn't so.'

"At first it didn't look like he intended to prove anything. He plodded along, letting the others show all the speed they wanted, for half a mile, one mile, mile and a half. Then, all of a sudden, he was off. I never saw such speed at a finish. He took the lead and was over the finish line almost before you knew he had begun to move. It was beautiful!"

A groom said, "I saw that race. You'd sure never forget it. Set a track record, didn't he?"

"Yes—he ran two miles in three minutes, twenty-one and four-fifths seconds. The record still stands." Mike laughed. "Pretty good for a horse that wasn't in condition."

Exterminator reached down and playfully tugged at Mike's sleeve. "Yes, we're talking about you." Mike rubbed the big head fondly.

"What about the time he beat the famous sprinter Billy Kelley in the Harford Handicap! That was a great race.'"

"Yes, sir. I'll never forget that one. Lots of folks thought Exterminator didn't have a chance against Billy Kelley—he was the most famous sprinter in the country. And the Harford Handicap was a sprint—just three-quarters of a mile. Billy Kelley had won it three years straight. His groom and I had an argument just before the race started, and I said, 'Take your nag back to the barn, boy—Exterminator has as good as won.' But I didn't feel as sure as I sounded. Then Old Bones was off like lightning, taking the lead from the famous sprinter, and across the finish line. Like there was nothing to it. He was seven years old then—most of the horses he'd raced with as a three-year-old had already been retired."

"He had a great year as a seven-year-old, didn't he?"

"Yes. I'd say his greatest. That was the year he won the Saratoga Cup for the fourth time. No other horse ever won the Saratoga Cup four years in succession. It's a hard race, too—mile and three quarters."

"Boy, I remember that day," an old-timer spoke up. "I was afraid he couldn't take it. For I'd seen him at Latonia the week before carrying a hundred and forty pounds. I figured he was too worn out with all the weight he'd been carrying to win the Saratoga Cup. But he won."

"The Pimlico Cup was another one Exterminator liked

to take—I remember seeing him and Boniface battle for that one—that's a race Henry McDaniel loves to talk about!"

"Sure, I remember that—"

"Remember the day they raced Exterminator against time, trying to find out how fast he could run under perfect conditions? The weather was perfect, the track fast, Exterminator at his peak. Lots of folks figured he would set a world speed record, without doubt. The jockey was dressed in the Kilmer silks, as he would be for a real race. Men were in the judges' stand, timers and starters ready. Exterminator loped off. He wasn't in any hurry at all. When he crossed the finish line he had made one of the slowest runs of his career. He looked at the empty grandstands, then at the men waiting, and he gave them a real horse laugh. He hadn't been fooled for a minute. Knew all the time it wasn't a race."

So they talked—recalling the old days, naming the great races, reliving the many victories, recounting the cups he had won.

Old Bones was never happier than when old friends came to visit. But he enjoyed all the other visitors too —the people who had never known him personally but had heard of him, perhaps had seen him race, and wanted to meet the famous thoroughbred.

He stood graciously, while they looked him over and talked about his glorious past. After the talk had gone on for a little while, he would whinny toward Peanuts, urging them to give the pony some attention, too. And the visitors always did.

Children came to visit him, too. Old Bones liked the

children. He would stand very quietly while Mike lifted a child up on his high back, then walk slowly around the paddock, with Mike leading him.

When the child was lifted down, Mike would say, laughing, "Now you're famous. Yes, sir. You can brag to your grandchildren that you once rode the great Exterminator."

Sometimes the children brought cubes of sugar, apples, and carrots for Old Bones. He would be careful to take them neatly and gently from their fingers, so that even the smallest children were not frightened by the great head reaching toward them, the wide jaws opening for the tidbit.

So the happy years went on.

There was only one major change in their lives. Mr. Kilmer died, and the farm in Virginia, with all its horses, was to be sold. All but Exterminator, Peanuts, and Sun Briar. In his will Mr. Kilmer provided that these three should never be sold. They were to live on another beautiful Kilmer farm in New York State, near Binghamton. Mr. Kilmer left plenty of money so that they would have the finest care, the best of everything, as long as they lived.

Old Bones had stayed on the New York farm many times when he was still racing. He was happy there. And Peanuts liked it, too. Mike Terry went with them, of course, and life went on just as pleasantly and comfortably as it had before.

Every year, when spring rolled around, preparations began for Old Bones' birthday party.

Now, in Binghamton, everyone connected with the Kilmer farm was getting ready for the biggest birthday party Old Bones had ever had. On the thirtieth of May Exterminator would be twenty-nine years old. That is very old for a horse. It is equal to about ninety years of age for a human being.

All the children from Binghamton and the neighboring countryside were invited to the party.

On the day of the party Mike Terry brushed and combed Old Bones, brushed and combed until Old Bones snorted with impatience and grabbed Mike's coat sleeve in his teeth. Enough was enough!

Another groom, Bill, brushed and combed Peanuts until Peanuts squealed with impatience.

Mike brought yards and yards of narrow satin ribbon, green, orange, and brown, into the barn. He said, "You're going to wear the Kilmer colors again today, Old Bones. Not the way you used to—but you're going to wear them."

Patiently Mike braided the silken ribbons into Old Bones' mane, and tied them in bows. He gave Bill what was left over for Peanuts.

When he had Old Bones all fixed up for the birthday party, Mike said, "You look fine, old boy. Of course, you're growing old, and you're getting fat. But, then, I've put on some weight, too—and I'm not as young as I used to be either." He rubbed Old Bones' head affectionately, and Old Bones reached down to nuzzle Mike. Then he whinnied happily, for there was excitement in the air, and he knew this day was special.

Soon cars and buses rolled up to the Kilmer home, and children began piling out. Old Bones, with Peanuts at his heels, ran happily to the fence to greet them. He stood proudly while they admired him in his birthday finery, and leaned his head over the fence so that they could pet him.

They begged Mike for rides. Mike said, "Exterminator is old now, and he'll get tired if many of you ride. We'll let three or four of the littlest children ride him, but that's all."

The children understood. They agreed. They watched Mike while he put the smallest ones on Old Bones' back and led the horse slowly around the paddock.

The children petted Peanuts and laughed at the touch of his wet little nose nuzzling them. They laughed when Old Bones grabbed Mike's coat collar and tugged at it and Mike skinned out of the jacket, letting Exterminator hold it. With delight they watched Old Bones chase Peanuts across the paddock and Peanuts nip at his old friend's legs.

Some of the older children asked, "May we see the trophies, please?" And Mrs. Kilmer took them into the special room that was filled with all the silver cups and beautiful trophies Exterminator had won during his years of racing.

Mike Terry rang the bell, and everyone gathered around Old Bones and Peanuts.

Then from the barn came Mike, proudly carrying the huge birthday cake he had made for Old Bones.

It was beautiful! It was made of ground-up apples, corn, bran, and oats. Twenty-nine golden carrot candles trimmed it. Best of all, Old Bones and Peanuts could eat it.

Mrs. Kilmer had chocolate cake and ice cream for the children.

Together they all sang:

"Happy birthday to you, happy birthday to you. Happy birthday, Old Bones. . . . Happy birthday to you."

Mrs. Kilmer made a little speech. She told the children how nice it had been to have them come to the party. She told them "Thank you" for the gifts of apples and candy and sugar cubes they had brought. She told them the reason Old Bones looked so fit at his great old age was that Mike Terry had given him such excellent and loving care through all the years.

Then Mike took a bow and told the children how he had met Old Bones twenty-six years earlier, in the barn with Mr. McDaniel, just before the Derby. And how he had said then that he would never leave him, and he never had.

The children cheered Mike; they cheered Old Bones and Peanuts.

It was time for the children to go. "Good-by, Old Bones. . . . Good-by, Peanuts. . . . Happy birthday, Old Bones. . . . Good-by, Mike Terry. . . . Thank you. . . . It was a lovely party, Mrs. Kilmer. Thank you . . . thank you. . . ."

Old Bones stood at the fence and watched the children go. He whinnied after them. He wished they could stay longer. He had loved his party. Even though he was tired now with all the celebrating, he did not want the party to end.

A neighbor boy ran back to reach up and give Old Bones one last pat. He said, "Mrs. Kilmer, may we have a party for Old Bones again next year, with all the children? Please?"

Mrs. Kilmer hesitated. She looked at Exterminator. He was very old. Did she dare promise? Old Bones looked at her. It was a long, wise look from the eyes with hazel color. Then he winked slowly.

Mrs. Kilmer smiled and said, "Yes, Danny. We will have another party for Old Bones next year."

And they did.

These are the facts in the life of the great horse
EXTERMINATOR, *affectionately known as* OLD BONES.

Born May 30, 1915, at the W. D. Knight farm, near Lexington, Kentucky. Dam, Fair Empress. Sire, McGee.

An unknown in 1918, he won the Kentucky Derby. He went on to become America's top winner of cup races and, many claim, the greatest thoroughbred ever developed in this country.

Retired in 1924, at the age of nine, when he pulled up lame in his 100th race.

Died in 1945 at the ripe old age of thirty. Exterminator is buried on the Kilmer farm, near Binghamton, New York, beside his constant companion, the pony Peanuts II, and near his old stablemate, Sun Briar.